NEW BRUNSWICK

JOURNEY ACROSS CANADA

Harry Beckett

The Rourke Book Co., Inc.
Vero Beach, Florida 32964

Harry Beckett M.A. (Cambridge), M.Ed. (Toronto), Dip.Ed. (Hull, England) has taught at the elementary and high school levels in England, Canada, France, and Germany. He has also travelled widely for a tour operator and a major book company.

Edited by Laura Edlund
Laura Edlund received her B.A. in English literature from the University of Toronto and studied Writing for Multimedia and Book Editing and Design at Centennial College. She has been an editor since 1986 and a traveller always.

ACKNOWLEDGMENTS
For photographs: Geovisuals (Kitchener, Ontario), The Canadian Tourism Commission and its photographers.
For reference: *The Canadian Encyclopedia, Encarta 1997, The Canadian Global Almanac, Symbols of Canada. Canadian Heritage*, Reproduced with the permission of the Minister of Public Works and Government Services Canada, 1997.
For maps: Promo-Grafx of Collingwood, Ont., Canada.

Library of Congress Cataloging-in-Publication Data

Beckett, Harry. 1936 -
    New Brunswick / by Harry Beckett.
        p. cm. — (Journey across Canada)
    Includes index.
    ISBN 1-55916-202-3 (alk. paper)
    1. New Brunswick—Juvenile literature.
I. Title II. Series: Beckett, Harry, 1936 -   Journey across Canada : 12.
F1042.4.B43   1997
971.5'1—dc21   97–932
                                                        CIP
                                                        AC

Printed in the USA

TABLE OF CONTENTS

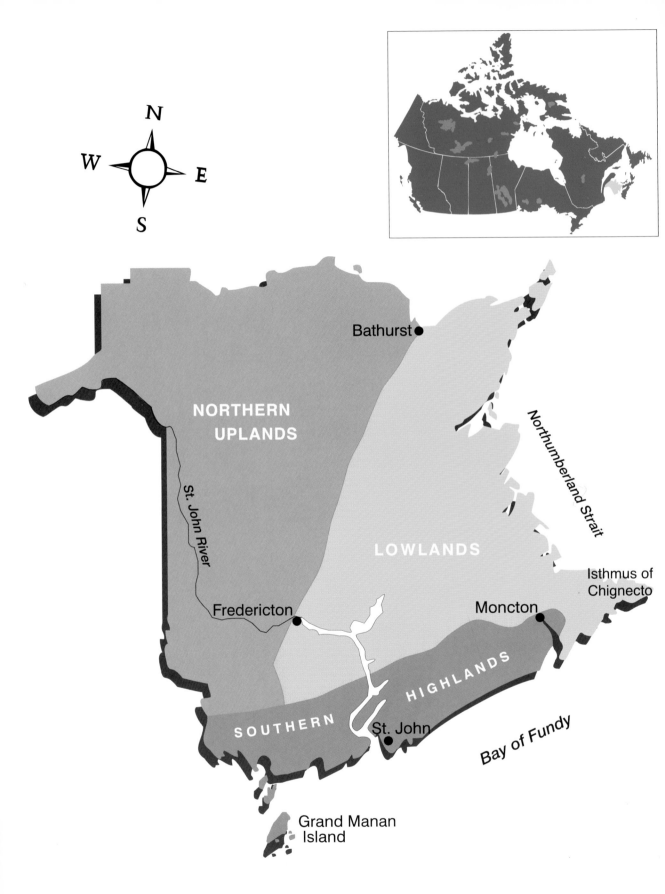

N
W E
S

Bathurst •

NORTHERN
UPLANDS

St. John River

LOWLANDS

Northumberland Strait

Isthmus of
Chignecto

Fredericton •

Moncton •

HIGHLANDS

SOUTHERN

St. John •

Bay of Fundy

Grand Manan
Island

PROVINCE OF NEW BRUNSWICK

Chapter One
SIZE AND LOCATION

New Brunswick lies on Canada's east coast, and is one of the **Maritimes** (MARE ih timez). It is joined to its southeastern neighbour, Nova Scotia, by a narrow neck of land.

To the south of this neck, Nova Scotia and New Brunswick share the Bay of Fundy. To its north, the Northumberland Strait separates New Brunswick from Prince Edward Island.

New Brunswick is one of Canada's smallest provinces. It is bordered to the north by the largest province, Québec. To the west is an American neighbour, the state of Maine.

From north to south, New Brunswick measures 400 kilometres (249 miles), and it is 370 kilometres (230 miles) from east to west.

Find out more...

- New Brunswick has 73 400 square kilometres (28 357 square miles) of land.
- The narrow neck of land is called the Isthmus of Chignecto.
- The Strait is about 15 kilometres wide.

Chapter Two

GEOGRAPHY: LAND AND WATER

New Brunswick is 83% forest, and 2% inland water. The northern uplands are rugged mountains. The centre and east of the province are rolling high land.

The lowlands form a triangle, with its corners at Bathurst in the northeast, Fredericton in the southwest, and Moncton in the east. South of the triangle lie a chain of sharp hills.

A river cutting its valley through the hilly interior

The east is low and flat. Note the irregular coastline.

The province's many rivers have formed deep valleys. There is little farmland and it lies mainly in these valleys. The major cities and most of the towns and villages were built in these valleys, too.

New Brunswick's coast has cliffs, bays, inlets, and fine beaches. The Northumberland Strait is shallow and warm, with fast-moving tides. The Bay of Fundy has the world's highest tides.

Chapter Three

WHAT IS THE WEATHER LIKE?

New Brunswick has hot summers and cold winters. On the coast, these are influenced by the winds that blow off the ocean. The climate is the most extreme away from the coast, especially in the northwest and centre of the province, where the land is high.

A lot of the **precipitation** (prih sip ih TAY shun) in the north falls as snow. Near the coast, only 15 to 20% of the precipitation is snow. Saint John, on the southern coast, has more precipitation than in the north, and it falls in about equal amounts in summer and in winter. The city has 106 days of fog every year and 173 days of frost.

Find out more...

- The climate in most of New Brunswick is called a continental climate.
- The average temperatures are -7.8°C (17° F) in January and 16.9°C (62° F) in July in Saint John.

Sailing on a fine summer's day off Shediac

Chapter Four

MAKING A LIVING: HARVESTING THE LAND

In the days of wooden ships, New Brunswick trees were used to make planks and masts. Now, the wood is made mostly into pulp and paper. Logs are still floated down the rivers from the middle of New Brunswick.

There are few fertile areas but most are in the Saint John River valley. The marshes around the Bay of Fundy have been drained so that farmers can farm them. A fifth of Canada's potatoes are grown in New Brunswick, and dairy farming is important as well. Most agricultural produce is used in the province.

Fishing brought the early settlers to the area. This industry has lost importance, but there are still good catches off the east coast and in the Bay of Fundy.

Logs being pushed, and pulled, to a pulp and paper mill

Find out more...

- Potatoes are exported, often as seed potatoes—which are used to grow other potatoes.
- People fish for lobster, crab, and herring off New Brunswick's coast.

When the first French settlers, the **Acadians** (uh KAY dee unz), settled along the Bay of Fundy and in the Saint John River valley, they were met and helped by **Micmac** (MIK mak) and later, **Malecite** (mal ih SEET) peoples.

In 1755, Britain gained control of the area, and forced out the Acadians. British and American **immigrants** (IM uh grunts) began to settle the area.

A two-horsepower engine cutting wood

Dried fish was important to the early Acadians.

After the American Revolution (1775-83), 14 000 **Loyalists** (LOY uh lists) arrived to settle mainly in the Saint John River area. Returning Acadians and some settlers from Québec went to the north and east.

The English-speaking and French-speaking communities have kept their different languages, cultures, and religions. The two languages have equal standing in the province.

The province's population includes about 15 000 Native people.

Chapter Six

MAKING A LIVING: FROM INDUSTRY

Finding good sites for manufacturing plants in New Brunswick is difficult because of its hills and forests. But it is the forests, sea, and land that supply the province's wealth.

People who work in manufacturing work mainly with wood and food. The raw materials are sometimes sold untreated and later sold back to the province as finished goods.

Recently, important mineral deposits have been found. New Brunswick coal, imported oil and the many rivers are used to generate electricity.

New Brunswick has other industries, such as shipbuilding and construction, which use local materials.

Government, education, transportation, and tourism employ almost eight out of ten New Brunswickers.

Find out more...

- Other minerals here are zinc, silver, lead, copper, and gold.
- The province's power system is linked to Québec, Nova Scotia, Prince Edward Island, and New England in the U.S.

A major food processing plant in Florenceville

Chapter Seven

IF YOU GO THERE...

You can see the Reversing Falls on the Saint John River as it flows into the Bay of Fundy. Twice a day, the tidal waters rush in so quickly that they flow upstream, over low waterfalls.

Near Moncton, on Magnetic Hill, cars seem to roll up hill, because of an **optical** (OP tih kul) **illusion** (ih LOO zhun).

The past lives again at Kings Landing, the Acadian Historical Village, the old French fort of Beauséjour, and the summer home of Franklin Delano Roosevelt on Campobello Island.

There is hunting and fishing in northern New Brunswick, and in winter, skiing. Summer tourists love the beaches and even kayaking among whales.

Young people in Loyalist dress at Kings Landing

Find out more...

- Kings Landing is a restored Loyalist settlement.
- Roosevelt was the thirty-second President of the United States.

17

Chapter Eight

MAJOR CITIES

Fredericton, the capitol of New Brunswick, is a small, friendly city 135 kilometres (84 miles) inland on the Saint John River. It is a city of government, trade, and tourism. The University of New Brunswick is an important part of life there.

The Legislative Building in Fredericton

In the harbour at Saint John

The province's largest city is Saint John. First settled in 1630, it has a busy pulp and paper industry, shipbuilding, and port facilities. The Fundy tides keep its port free of ice all winter.

Rail lines in the Maritimes and from Maine pass through Moncton. It is a shipbuilding, manufacturing, and agricultural centre on the Petitcodiac River. A third of the people speak French.

Chapter Nine

SIGNS AND SYMBOLS

The flag shows the golden lion of Britain at the top. The ship and waves, below, represent the importance of shipbuilding and the sea in New Brunswick's history.

The coat of arms shows the lion, ship, and sea again on a shield. Beside, the white-tailed deer are wearing the Union Jack and the fleur-de-lis hanging from collars of Native beads showing the province's British, French, and Native histories. There are royal crowns (one with gold maple leaves), an Atlantic salmon, fiddlehead ferns, and the provincial flower also on the coat of arms.

The Latin motto means "Hope restored."

The provincial flower is the purple violet, which grows very well in New Brunswick.

New Brunswick's flag, coat of arms, and flower

GLOSSARY

Acadians (uh KAY dee unz) — the people of the former French colony in eastern Canada; their descendants

immigrant (IM uh grunt) — a person who comes to another country or region to live

Loyalist (LOY uh list) — people of the American colonies who sided with Britain in the American Revolution

Malecite (mal ih SEET) — a Native people living in New Brunswick, eastern Québec, Maine

Maritimes (MARE ih timez) — New Brunswick, Prince Edward Island, and Nova Scotia; named so because they are on the sea

Micmac (MIK mak) — a Native people of eastern Canada

optical illusion (OP tih kul ih LOO zhun) — something that people see in a way that gives a false idea

precipitation (prih sip ih TAY shun) — rain, dew, or snow

There are many covered bridges in New Brunswick

INDEX